Titles by *Lan...*

Rock of God

(Kilán ke Nyùy)

JK Bannavti

Langaa Research & Publishing CIG
Mankon, Bamenda

Publisher:
Langaa RPCIG
Langaa Research & Publishing Common Initiative
Group
P.O. Box 902 Mankon
Bamenda
North West Region
Cameroon
Langaagrp@gmail.com
www.langaa-rpcig.net

Distributed outside N. America by African Books
Collective
orders@africanbookscollective.com
www.africanbookscollective.com

Distributed in N. America by Michigan State
University Press
msupress@msu.edu
www.msupress.msu.edu

ISBN: 9956-616-05-2

DISCLAIMER

The names, characters, places and incidents in this book are either the product of the author's imagination or are used fictitiously. Accordingly, any resemblance to actual persons, living or dead, events, or locales is entirely one of incredible coincidence.

Contents

Dedication

To Helen, Moala, Bamnjo and Nfii

Acknowledgement

I want to express deep appreciation to Shey-wantoh Caroline Asogha-Shemlon for the painstaking effort she made to review the script and to Shey Stephen Shemlon for encouraging me to forage in the history of Nso "because there is enough material in that history to write several kinds of works." It has been more than a rewarding experience.

Historical Context of *Rock of God*

Rock of God is a product of an invaluable experience growing up as part of a family whose history in the Nso kingdom is built around chivalry, conquest and unalloyed allegiance to the kingdom. The story centres on a significant war that Nso fought with Bamoun in the 1880s, and which war resulted in a devastating defeat for the Bamouns. During this war, a major Nso combat rule was broken: the Sultan (king) of Bamoun was decapitated. Both local story tellers and historians have indicated that the Sultan was only supposed to be captured alive. Some of the reasons for this are very compelling:

The first reason is that the two kingdoms were founded by siblings, that is, brother and sister born by the same king and queen-mother of the Tikar dynasty. As a result, and in spite of the hostility that might have characterized their relationship, there was an interest in avoiding self bereavement. In fact Fon Sehm II (1875-1907), is reported to have wept in public when the head of his "brother" the Sultan of the Bamouns was presented to him on a spear. He actually cursed Bukap (or Kpukov) with leprosy for violating his order which was to "teach my brother a lesson» and not «send him to the ancestors". Bukap is said to have died rejoicing because he saved Nso from the Bamouns.

The second reason (seen to be more general) is that a captured king was a prized trophy that could be used to extract necessary concessions during treaty negotiations. Since the Bamouns had become quite a thorn in the Nso flesh, a captured sultan would have been invaluable in arm-twisting the opponent at the end of the war.

Unfortunately the Sultan got killed in that war by ViSov fighting under Manjong Bah: ViSov became part of the Nso Kingdom in the early part of the 16th century when after the death of the Fon of Tabesov in Ngveh, a succession crisis arose between SEH, the rightful heir and another claimant. SEH and his followers were compelled to leave Tabesov, Ngveh and head out south in search of sanctuary. The Fon of Nso welcomed them and provided land and territory to settle. Because of this magnanimity, it seemed Visov always looked for opportunities to demonstrate loyalty to the Nso crown: They performed their duties too well - guarding the southern frontiers and staving off any invasion from that end. Kingdom security was so important to them that they at times cared less about the rules of war. This was largely the underlying factor in the decapitation of the Sultan of the Bamouns.

Nso and Bamoun had been constantly quibbling, and to many, this seemed to be mostly sibling rivalry than any unavoidable conflict. Since Nso was founded by the sister (Ngon Nso), the brother (Nchare-Yen, founder of Bamoun) always saw himself as the successor to the throne of Nso, according to the Tikar tradition that they both knew and respected. This may explain why Ngon-Nso never became Fon herself when she brought the Mtaar clan under her control and expanded the size of the kingdom. Instead she acted as regent for her son who was still growing up. Furthermore she signed a pact with the Mtaar that led to the elaboration of the monarchy the way we have it today. Rules of succession in the kingship of Nso are based on this pact.

Several generations passed and time seemed to have provided the necessary antidote to the anger and frustration between the two kingdoms. Nso and Bamoun decided to reconstruct their relationship in the middle 1900s. The birth years of modern Cameroon (1960 and 1961) saw the rise of President Ahmadou Ahidjo whose mother was from Bamoun. Although there is no clear evidence that Ahidjo might have pushed for a rapprochement between the two kingdoms, it has been argued that he hoped the close relationship would provide an indispensable bridge to his Cameroon Unification agenda. There is also evidence that between 1945-1960 when the Nso kingdom was part of British Cameroons, and Bamoun was part of French Cameroons, the two kingdoms were further separated by the two western super cultures. The effect of this was partly that Nso and Bamoun kingdoms had a chance to focus on other priorities thus cooling off enormously from the animosity that had become their leitmotif. When negotiations later resumed, the return of the Sultan's skull was a prized element in the negotiation.

A key player in the negotiations to return the Sultan's skull to the Bamouns was Sehm III (Mbinkar Mbinglo), who reigned as Paramount Fon of Nso from 1947 to 1972. As a young prince, Mbinglo's thirst for the throne was so overtly expressed that in 1910 it stymied the relationship between him and his uncle Ngah Bifon I (1910-1947) who was enthroned. Rather than eliminate Mbinkar Mbinglo for exhibiting naked usurpation of power, the newly enthroned Ngah Bifon I sent his nephew on "exile". Mbinkar Mbinglo sought refuge in Bamoun under Sultan Njoya Ibrahim (1889-1933). It was here that the young prince matured, almost as a "step-brother" to Seydou Njimolouh Njoya who later became Sultan of the Bamouns (1933-1992). Mbinkar Mbinglo is understood to have made a pact with Seydou Njimolouh Njoya that if he (Mbinglo) were ever to become Paramount Fon of Nso, he would return Njoya's grandfather's skull for proper burial. Seydou Njoya became Sultan in 1933. Fourteen years later in 1947, Mbinkar Mbinglo became Paramount Fon of Nso. His "brother" Seydou Njoya came over for his enthronement and reminded him of this accord. But the institutional framework of Nso did not make it easy for the Fon to live up to the accord. Sehm III (Mbinkar Mbinglo) spent his political life trying to convince Nwerong and Manjong to honour the deal with Seydou Njimolouh Njoya. It took until 1970 for the deal to be sealed.

Rock of God is also about the process of knowledge transfer in a non-literate context. Children who grew up very close to their elders benefited tremendously from the local story telling tradition by receiving useful information on morality, social responsibility, structure and expectations. They had the unique opportunity to be in close contact with both the story tellers and the object of the story. This was true for the myths as it was for major historical events and encounters.

Kilan Ké Nyuy, is part of this mythic past of Nso. This rock sat on a low-lying plateau in Ngewir (final 'r' is pronounced) on the foot of the Shiy hill, along the Jakiri-Foumban highway. It was a huge and those who trekked to Ber (final 'r' is pronounced) said it lay in majestic silence and evoked a sense of awe. But no one had a story about the rock apart from the fact that this was "God's rock." So it must be! In the world of this play, it has come to serve as the rallying platform of the land; a source of truth, honour and reverence; a seat of the Mighty Builder from whose vantage point we can project to the future while retaining the ability to look back at how far we have travelled. It is the fertile ground on which wisdom grows and progeny prospers, but at the same time a cemetery for selfishness, truthlessness and lawlessness. And true to form, this rock was uniquely named Kilan Ké Nyuy, meaning rock of God, from which the play gets its title.

Noteworthy too is the fact that within the fabric of the story, the Lamnso proverb has not only lived its authoritative depth and breath, it has provided the context for both legend and myth to come alive. For instance, we are thrust into the multidimensional implications of the rainbow in the foreground while following through on the pronouncement of the Rock, and the migratory trail from Tikar in the background. Over this maze is the Mighty threat that hangs over the land of Bamkov as lineage heads plot the disappearance of the sealed bag. This enhances a cultural complexity that defies compartmentalization as it evolves so convincingly on a belief system that impacts the daily existence of the people.

Shey Stephen Shemlon (PhD)

Dramatis Personae

Ngaiwir	Elder of the family
Tatah	Son of Tabesov
Menang	Son of Ngaiwir
Fon	King of Bamkov
Yewong	Guardian of the kingdom's sacred duties and rules
Tawong	Guardian of the Kingdom's sacred shrines and rules
Ndzev	Lead Councillor
Maa	Councillor
Faa	Councillor
Mbing	Councillor with special execution duties
Mformi Bah	Manjong war lead
Mformi Gham	Manjong war lead
Gwei	Herald and spokesman of the Rock
Tav	Suitor to Ngon
Sultan	King of Momban
Mefiri	Lead councillor to the Sultan
Mbombo	Momban war Lead
Ngon	Princess of Momban
Mopete	Praise singer
Matapi	Councillor to the Sultan
Mominyi	Advisor to the Sultan
Drummers and crowd of dancers	

1

Act One

Scene One

(Night: Heavy growling noise rumbles off in succession creating an atmosphere of fright and eerie expectation. Gwei's dreamy voice comes faintly across. He sounds urgent, but also very exhausted and deliberate.)

The Rock of God[1] has spoken.
But we are all too drunk, all too busy!
Oh headless Bamkov, let your king oblige!
Allow him do as the Rock has asked him.
Oh headless people!
Why do you have ears yet block them?
Why do you have eyes yet shut them?
The Mighty Rock is still spitting anger.
Here is word for you, people of this land.
Let the foreign king out of your hands!
Why are you keeping a departed fon[2]?

(Pauses, then almost stammering)

You won the war[3] and had the pumpkin,
But rather than harvest it, you uprooted it.
In your vengeance, you ruined the seed:
You broke the rule!
Now the fury of the Rock is on your trail.
Send out the foreign king for proper burial,
Else famine will swoop down on you like a hawk,
And the sky will descend to tangle up the earth!
Tawong[4] , are you listening to me?
Our sun will disappear behind a dark cloud
If we do not send the brother fon home!
Bamkov still belongs to the fon and Nwerong[5]
And truth will rule!
If we do not bow to the truth,
We will beat the throne[6] to get justice
When the Mighty Builder of the Rock strikes!

5

(Screams of pain and eerie sounds fade into chirps of birds announcing the beginning of early dawn. Scene opens up at a clearing in a flat piece of land on the foot of a plateau; a luxuriant fig tree beaming with green leaves is prominent in the foreground. A few shrubs grow by the side. Greenery around shows it is early rainy season. Chirping of morning birds and cock-crows remind us that life is just waking up. An old man, Ngaiwir[7], wearing beads over a jumper shirt and carrying a scabbard and a spear, stands at the foot of a fig tree. He is followed by two young boys about ten and twelve. They are also carrying a calabash fuming with early morning palm wine. Ngaiwir takes the calabash and positions it at the foot of the tree. He steps back to the children and then walks slowly pointing to the stem of the big fig tree. The boys' gaze in the direction of Ngaiwir's pointing finger is very unwavering.)

Ngaiwir

It was here!
(Shakes his head as he reminisces)

Menang

What, old one?

Ngaiwir

It was here it all happened!

Tatah

What happened?

Ngaiwir

The battle of Fafem[8] in the war between Momban and Bamkov
This was the height of the war!
The battle blades sparkled in the air
Like lightning flashing in the dark rainy night.
The clashing machetes echoed in the air
Like a stream of double bells hit in fright.

(Ngaiwir executes a manjong war dance mimicking some of the fighting that took place)

Manjong[9] warriors shuffled their way like soldier ants
In the undergrowth, from Mbisha' to Fafem.
Infrequent horns of manjong tore the darkness
Sending coded messages to holed up women and
children,
That unless the sky crashed on the earth[10]
Their future would bloom like the fig tree on Tavirerr
hill.

The air hung heavily over the land
As spears hissed through the savannah,
Swooshing down enemies
Like sharp lances on young banana stems.
Mumbled groans told you it was a wound
But long groans meant it was over.

Then came the magic moment!
Gwei Bukap[11], son of Tabesov,
Son of the leopard hunter,
Crawled in like a millipede[12]
Surprising his majesty -
His majesty the prey of Momban!

Tatah
So what did he do?
Ngaiwir
Bukap rose out of the millipede
And growled at his majestic prey
With dripping fury,
And yawning hunger.
Four or five times he darted
Like his forefathers had done.

But I tell you children
Bukap was no ordinary man.
His spear buried every foe

And shrivelled leopard or lion!
Hardly would he dart more than once
Before releasing his spiky messenger of death.

Like a sun bird he swung to the left,
And like a dazzler he skirted around,
Until his crowned enemy started tilting
And drooling like the victim of epilepsy,
Mumbling and chewing his tongue,
Before dropping on all fours.

This enemy was no common enemy:
The enemy was lion;
Stem of the rainbow!
Elephant!
Roar of the forest!
The enemy was king!

But there he was,
Shivering like a thieving dog
Puking up a stolen bone.
There crawled the lonesome crown of Momban
Blown from his heath by the hurricane
And left naked in the open field.

Here he was, struggling against
Bukap's snarl of vengeance.
King of the fiercest fighters under the sun
Begging a termite for his breath
But knowing the end had come
To him who once was lion.

Oh merciless life,
How cruel of you
To hack down the mighty so ruthlessly

Reducing them to paupers and beggars!
If you were man, I would call a feast
On the day your own death comes.

Bukap leaned back like an arc
And released the spear of death.
It planted the royal body on the tree trunk
Releasing a torrent of royal blood.
The sultan's cry of pain drowned the woods,
And the royal head drooped forward.

With his merciless machete
Gwei swung forward
And plucked for his bag of war
A rich harvest for his clan
And Manjong songs rent the air
As it trooped uphill to the palace.

Manjong Gham crossed from Liv[13]
And burnt to the ground
The palace of the enemy,
Looting girls[14] and goods
In show of ravenous victory.

Tatah
So everyone gathered in the palace
Even with girls they stole from enemy land?
Menang
Do not disturb the story!
What kind of stupid question is that?

Ngaiwir
Actually, Tatah is right, but we will get to that later.
Manjong sang its way in coiled circles
Until the entire palace arena was filled,

Hitting the blunt tails of the spears in unison
While spiky spear heads pointed skywards
In readiness to wear the crown of victory.

Gwei's horn announced the king.
His majesty heaved a ritual cough
And out of the bulging bags of war
Victors pulled out kills from the war,
And planted them on top of the spears;
A proof that it was certain victory.

His Majesty stepped out in peacock feathers.
He lifted his face and lifted his gun
To fire the land to a joyous start.
But behold right in front of him,
Sitting on the sharp teeth of Bukap's spear
Was the sightless head of his brother!

"Oh sky fall on me!"[15] screamed the King
Dropping his gun without a shot
But with a loud certain thud,
Sending the crowd into naked silence.
And one could hear a pin drop
For a king had lost a king

A brother king is king
Born of the same royal blood
On the same leopard skin[16]
By the same aboriginal queen[17]
And must be interred with his forebears
In the royal cemetery.

This was the saddest victory we ever won.
We wage wars to protect ourselves
Not to spill our own blood.

(Pauses and resumes softly)
But children, it was here it all began:
Here under this tree, along this Fafem stretch
Your family was the cause of our joy and pain.

Menang
So what did the Fon do to Gwei? Did he punish him?
Ngaiwir
Yes, His Majesty was boiling in anger,
But did only what a Fon could do.
Menang
What?
Ngaiwir
He knighted Gwei.
How can you beat your child
And thank him at the same time?
The Fon found the answer.
Tatah
What was it?
Ngaiwir
Beat him and thank him at the same time.
Menang
I am confused.
Ngaiwir
You should be.
You will understand when you grow.
(He walks forward, and then suddenly stops.)
You all will one day find heavy loads on your
shoulders.
On behalf of your family and this Kingdom,
You must never put the load down.
You can never put the load down!
Tatah
Well if the load is heavy I will put it down to drink
some water at least.

11

Menang

I will too.

Ngaiwir

That is true,
But then you pick it up and keep going.
You must stay on duty.
We all grow into it.
Do you hear me?

Tatah

Yes

Menang

Yes

Ngaiwir

Another thing: You, the young generation,
You are very noisy about what your forefathers did
And what you yourselves have done.
A wise hunter does not shuffle the grass to taunt the
lion;
He lets the wind do it.
A leopard does not announce its spots;
It is known by them.
A chick does not chirp when the hawk hovers above;
It just realizes danger is near.
Get up; let us make sure we get to the Rock on time.

Tatah

My legs are tired.

Menang

Mine too.

Ngaiwir

Even after you have rested this long?
Don't complain like children who have eaten porridge.

Menang

I remember you said this Fon of Momban was a
brother to our Fon. His people must therefore be our
people. How come we were fighting them?

Ngaiwir

You will have the answer to those questions today.
Today is that big day in the land:
It is victory day!
It is the day our clan planted its fig tree[18]:
The day we cut our tooth!
The day we shut up the world!
That is the day Ngon found her voice.

On our victory day
All is swept and clean
Fresh air cuddles the land
And palm wine, kola nut and food
Are shared by smiling victors.
No woman goes to the farm
No man goes to the bush.
It is victory day!

It is the day we tell the story as it happened:
How we as a people came to be here.
This is the day Nwerong visits the four corners of the
Kingdom
Marking its foot print with freshly shattered raffia
stalk;
Then it returns to the Rock of God to authorize ritual
festivities.
It is the day we honour the Mighty One at His Rock
For conquering our foes for us.
This is the biggest day in this Kingdom.
Let us hasten up.

Tatah

Hey, look at that arc in the sky. This is surely going to
be a magnificent day.

Menang
Yes, the rainbow! It is shiny. So what boa constrictor[19] has spat it out into the sky? I am sure the boa must have swallowed several deer and is just laying tired and heavy now.

Tatah
Let us go over there and shoot the boar with our spears.

(Ngaiwir continues to scan the rainbow and listen intently. Then he hurries the children away as approaching voices become a little louder. He seems to know them.)

Very important voices are approaching!
Let us hurry away!

Exit

Notes

1. Rock of God:
   Loosely translated from Kilán ké Nyùy in Lamnso'. Lamnso is a language spoken by the people of Nso kingdom in northwestern Cameroon. Kilán ké Nyùy is a huge rock in Ngewir village on the Jakiri-Foumban highway. The title of this play comes from the name of that rock. The reason for which the rock was named 'Rock of God' is based on the local belief that God was present in the rock: No explanation is available except the fact that the rock inspired fright and awe by sheer force of its size and the 'majestic' silence surrounding it. This concept of God here is different from that of the gods that are generally said to occupy other elements of nature such as lakes and waterfalls etc.

2. Fon:
   Fon or king. The two words are used interchangeably in northwestern Cameroon. The word is part of the Cameroonian English lexicon. Its adaptation into the local English is evident in various forms of usage: Examples include fondom for kingdom, fonship for kingship, and other derivatives.

3. Won the war:
   This refers to the Nso-Bamun war that was fought in the 1800s and which resulted in the decapitation of the sultan (the king) of the Bamuns. The enemy king was supposed to be captured and brought to the Nso palace alive because he is a brother to the king of Nso. The founder of the Bamun kingdom Nchare-Yen and the founder of the Nso kingdom, Ngon-Nso, were prince and princess born by the same king and queen of the Tikar dynasty.

15

6. Beat the throne:

The Nso people utilize the throne of their monarch as an instrument of justice. In the event that they are unable to have culprits confess their guilt, everyone involved in the dispute could be required to lay their hands on the throne and declare their innocence. It is understood that once the guilty falsely declare innocence, they are visited by death or other form of catastrophe. Many people who are guilty hardly accept to beat the throne. They rather just confess the truth.

7. Ngaiwir:

Literally, old one, or older one. It is an honorific expression for an elderly man. It is also the equivalent of the title of Shey in some lineages or clans. In large families such as Ndzendzev, Sov (Tabesov, Sop, Sob) and Tsenla Kikai, Ngaiwir could be used for the next in line to Shufai who is the head of the lineage and advisor to the fon.

8. Fafem:

A stretch of semi-level land southeast of Jakiri, (Mantum Palace) on the Jakiri-Foumban highway.

9. Manjong:

A military organization that includes all men of fighting age. Manjong is a unifying force for a network of organizations embedded in the highly stratified Nso military system. The two most prominent divisions of manjong are Manjong Ba' and Manjong Gham. They are responsible for the operational execution of war. See Verkijika Fanso and Bongfen Langhee in "Nso Military Organization and Warfare in the 19th and 20th Centuries" in *African Crossroads: Intersections Between History and Anthropology in Cameroon* Ian Fowler ed., Oxford, 1996; vol. 2, p 101-114.

10. Sky crashes on the earth:
    A metaphoric expression translated from Lamnso' referring to the moment when the impossible would happen. Similar expressions include: 'the sky tumbling to tangle up the earth' or 'when the sky descends to meet the earth'.

11. Gwei Bukap:
    Bukap is the name of the young man from Sop or Tabesov, or Sov who decapitated the   sultan of Bamun during the war between Bamun and Nso in the 1800s. He fought in the frontlines of Manjong Dzekwa, the military regiment assigned to attacks against the kingdom from the east.

12. Millipede:
    Legend holds that for Bukap to decapitate the sultan of Bamun, he magically converted himself into a millipede and crawled very close to the monarch before suddenly surprising his target.

13. Liv:
    The name of the river and village at the northeastern border of Nso and Bamoun kingdoms.

14. Girls:
    Nso is reported to have plundered the Bamun kingdom so terribly, arresting and seizing young girls and women in huge numbers. All of these were reportedly not killed or maltreated. They were brought to Nso alive, treated like family and married out to children and friends to boost the Nso population.

15. Sky fall on me:
    An expression which refers to the impossible that has happened. This should never have happened based on Nso rules of war, but anecdotal recounts say neither Bukap nor the entire Tabesov contingent knew any much about the Nso rules of war. They cared for nothing other than victory, and by all means necessary.

16. Leopard skin:

    Legend holds that the Fon's bed is sheeted in leopard skin. It also holds that the the rug the Fon steps on to climb into his bed is made of the skin (hide) of the leopard. Since the Fon is a prince, his mother had to step on the same rug and sleep with the king to conceive the reigning king.

17. Aboriginal queen:

    Historians record that when Ngon-Nso settled in Kovifem she made a pact with the aborigines in which it was stipulated that for a prince to become king, he must be born by a mother from the aboriginal stock.

18. Fig tree:

    Nso used the fig tree as a boundary marker. A fig true was particularly known for its resilience and longevity.

19. Boar constrictor:

    Many children's stories in Nso folklore attribute the source of the rainbow to the boar constrictor that 'spits it out into the sky'. This is often a sign that the boar has eaten a heavy meal such as a goat or a duika and cannot move.

    Another interpretation says that the rainbow is an astrological sign: once it forms around the sun, it is an indication that a very important or high ranking person is going to die. A similar concept says that a rainbow foreshadows a heavy downpour that could be devastating in many ways.

Scene Two

(Three men appear from behind the tree: They discuss the strategy of the Kingdom. Their tone is urgent)

Ndzev

Gham[1], look over there to your weak arm. Make sure they are gone. Are they?

Gham

From what I can see, they are not at ear shot

Ndzev

Look especially for the movement of the grass. Can you see any of them swaying over there?

Bah[2]

You sound like you are talking to young boys who are just learning tree climbing. *(Laughs)* This is our work!

Ndzev

Was that not something? I almost called out to salute Ngaiwir on passing down our history of conquest and achievement to the children. What a Way to put it! He is a story teller without compare.

Gham

I tell you it drove up my blood so much I almost hit the tree with my spear.

Bah

Once a warrior, always a warrior! Ngaiwir has no idea what he has done to me today. I feel like having a little battle before the major event. The only thing lacking is some Mentsengong[3] war medicine to get me started.

Ndzev

(Scanning the horizon) Have you seen that rainbow yet?

Bah

Yes, it is full with all the colours

Gham

I would have said it is a good indication that there will be no rain today.

But I cannot explain why my blood jumps up my left arm and even into my eye each time I look at it. Why should it seem so troubling on a day like this?

Bah

The warriors that we are should make sure we understand this quickly.

Ndzev

The first thing I would say is that it does not seem to be a good sign.

Although it is so bright in the air, it is very hazy around the sun.

Gham

Not good still. In fact it is worse if it swells around the sun.

If it stays hazy, that could just mean that we have a warning.

Well, manjong work is meant for any time signs are not good.

Ndzev

Valiant arms of our land.

You just said it, Gham.

Where are your cups?

(Serves them palm wine. The two stand and extend their cups to be served)

Calm your rising blood with the morning palm wine.

We are in the face of a challenge

And we must act like it is already here.

Gham

Yes I am waiting for the meat in your word.

Bah

Yes, the meat. Give us the meat!

What does the land want us to do?

Ndzev

First, I am happy you are seeing what I am seeing.
Our people say that the Fon has eight hundred eyes[4].
It is because in times like these
We comb every strand of hair in this land.
We sieve every river and every stream.
We clean the valleys and clear the mountains
We listen to every whistle in the passing wind
And catch every morsel at the border.
We make sure all is safe and secure
We stop the rain, and summon the sun.
So that our land savours the joys of its struggles

Bah

Father of the big Ndzev[5] clan,
If anything should rustle in Ngongbaah kov[6]
Or in the fishing swamps of Siy[7]
Manjong is ready to turn the place into dust.

Gham

Or if you tell us where the fire is burning,
Manjong is sure to do what only manjong does:
Put it out in no time.

Ndzev

There are no rain clouds yet.
There is no fire yet.
We just want to make sure that if…

Bah

Oh…if!

Gham

Oh…if!

(Regain their sitting position)

Ndzev

Yes, if….!
If Momban is entering our land showing a shinny face
But carrying a bag of soldier ants,

21

We should cut the bag right at the border.
If Momban greets us with soft hands
But offloads stinger bees,
We should have the antidote.
The Fon has eight hundred eyes!
Those eyes are yours and mine.

Bah

Yes Ndzev!

Gahm

Yes Ndzev!

Ndzev

Let me know which way the wind blows
Before, during and after the event.
Your cup is empty, Gham
(Pours him some palm wine)
And yours too Bah!
(Pours him some palm wine)
I will hurry to meet his majesty.
He is waiting.

(Ndzev exits. Gham and Bah Confer)

Bah

Did you see the look in his eyes?

Gham

What?

Bah

Never mind! Does the Fon know about this?

Gham

I do not doubt.

Bah

Something tells me he might not know.

Gham

You are Mformi. Are you not?

Bah

Is that in doubt?

Gham

Then find out for yourself.

Bah

That would bring confusion. It could tell Ndzev that I do not trust his word, and that is dangerous.

Gham

I agree. What would be the use asking? The task has all the evidence of love for the kingdom. Whether the Fon knows or not, does not matter. It is something he would not disagree with any way.

Bah

What do we do now?

Gham

Use our eyes. Open them very wide.

Bah

And increase them if possible.

Gham

Identify someone in their ranks.

Bah

A Bamkov man who is already part of the Momban family.

Gham

Certainly. But it could still be a Momban man.

Bah

If we had one.

Gham

Yes, if we had one.

Bah

I know one.

Gham

Of Momban?

Bah

No of course. Of Bamkov.

Gham

Who?

Bah

Tav!

Gham

They would easily fetch him out.

Bah

Why?

Gham

Because that is what he is, a Tav

Bah

No! He has been known as Tav since birth, so they think it is his name.

Gham

Even then, they may just play safe by not allowing him access to some places.

Bah

He does not need that. He is known there more than many of theirs. He has been living in Kupa Matapit for the last twenty years. He speaks Momban so well many of them have no idea he is from elsewhere.

Gham

The Name betrays him.

Bah

Anyone can name a child anything.

Gham

What does that mean? He could live there for the next hundred years; he would still be a Bamkov man. And you know how he brags about it.

Bah

Tav is our best hope. They trust him so much the princess of Momban has been betrothed to him. How do you think they would suspect him? He spends days in the palace of Momban paying his bride price.

Gham

His family is supposed to do that

Bah

I did not mean literally. What do you want me to call the so much hard work he does for the father of his would-be wife?

Gham

Any way, who of us would talk to him?

Bah

You do.

Gham

No, you do.

Bah

No, you do.

Gham

No, you.

Bah

Why?

Gham

Because you know him and his family.

Bah

But this is Tavnjong for goodness sake!

Gham

No, this is Tavnjong Fon.[8]

Bah

Still he issues from your division of manjong.

Gham

But this is not a manjong assignment.

Bah

Then what are we doing here?

Gham

Responding to the call of the land.

Bah

But that is what manjong does: kingdom security and war!

Gham

I know that!

Bah

So just get him to respond to the same call.

Gham

We are wasting time, Bah. Talk to Tav!

Bah

As a family friend or patriot?

Gham

As both.

Bah

Ha!

Gham

Anything else?

Bah

Certainly! How does he respond to us?

Gham

Give him your cup, and he will give it back.

Bah

All my cups are manjong cups. They will kill him when they see it.

Gham

Try another gift

Bah

That will still give room for suspicion.

Gham

I am not sure about that.

Bah

May be we wait for signs from his greeting.

Gham

How often shall he greet?

Bah

How would I know?

Gham

If he is unable to greet at all?

Bah

Just leave it to me. You will know when he talks to us.

Gham
Stand up. Take my machete.
Bah
Make sure there is still some palm wine in that calabash, else we might disappoint our God by not leaving any bit for the thirsty pregnant traveller.

(Both stand, pull out their machetes from the scabbards and clang, then turn their back to each other and exit in opposite directions. More voices are coming in as soon as these two leave. Someone is decidedly very annoyed and his voice echoes through the vegetation.)

Notes

1. Gham:
   Refers to Mformi Gham

2. Bah:
   Refers to Mformi Bah

3. Mentsengong:
   A name which seems breakable into the Nso phonological components of 'mentse'   blood, and 'ngòng' people as in 'mangong' which means mass populace. The combined word 'mentsengong' could mean something like 'blood of the people'. Mentsengong is a cult which legend holds developed some of the strongest magical potions that were used during the Nso wars to infiltrate enemy ranks. Mentsengong is   seated in the clan-head of Tabesov, the origin of Bukap, slayer of the sultan.

4. Eight hundred eyes:
   The saying in Lamnso, "the Fon has eight hundred eyes" refers to all human and institutional intelligence apparatus the Fon has at his disposal.

5. Ndzev:

   The head of the Ndzev clan is also referred to as Ndzev. This is a practice in Nso culture where rulers are sometimes addressed by the names of the places or families they represent.

6. Ngongbaah kov:

   Literally, Ngonbaah forest. A breakdown of the word into its Lamnso components suggests a forest where there are a lot of leopards. The forest used to be dense and thick according to local legend, and was always teaming with game. It therefore served as a fertile ground for hunting. Ngonbaah kov or Kov Ngonbaah is the Lamnso name for Kilum mountain forest in Oku.

7. Siy:

   Babesi, a border chieftain in the southern frontier of Nso. The people are referred to in Lamnso as Visiy.

8. Tavnjong Fon:

   Tavnjong is the leader of Njong, a squadron-type of group in the Nso military structure. Tavnjong Fon loosely means the fon's leader of Njong. Reference is to the patriotic responsibilities of Tavnjong as one who pays direct allegiance to the fon who is the Commander-in-chief of the kingdom.

Scene Three

(Enter a group of leaders and clan heads on their way to the Rock of God. They survey the area around the Ntamirr[1] and then sit down to cool off with some palm wine and get fresh air; one of them, Mbing, is rather restless)

Mbing

Whose idea was it that these Momban people should come for the event? This is not a day to waste waiting for a visitor.

Gwei

I understand your fear. But it seems the palace has more for today than we think.

(Hushed tones)

I hear we will be escorting the foreign king out of our land today. That makes the event even bigger than we thought.

Mbing

(Exasperated)

You heard from who? And who is the foreign king we had here?

Gwei

(Hushed)

Father of our big Mbing clan, give me your ear. What I heard is true. You of course know the foreign king I am referring to. Tawong and Yewong have been preparing the sealed-bag[2] of the land for the past several seasons.

Mbing

(Mimics)

They have been preparing… Tawong and Yewong …I hear….You hear from who?

Is the soil suddenly giving way under my foot or am I

29

still head of the Mbing clan and chief executioner like my forefathers? Where is Bamkov heading to?

Tawong

(Coming in and dropping his own bags to help. Mbing remains unmoved in his anger)

Calm down father of our Mbing family. This is the big day and whatever issues we have should be resolved calmly. The fighting already took place several years ago, and we are here to savour the juice of that war. What can I help our chief executioner with?

Mbing

(Fuming)

You have already prepared the sealed bag, have you not?

Tawong

The land has.

Mbing

What do you mean the land has?

Tawong

Because Yewong and I had to do it the way we do when our people honour the earth by keeping the majestic word.

Mbing

And then?

Tawong

And then we give the earth-mother in charge of fəm, the royal cemetery, the opportunity to hide the earth's gift where it belongs

Mbing

And where does it belong?

Tawong

In the fəm. But we had to transfer the sealed bag to where his majesty requested.

Mbing

Where?

Tawong

What? You want me to tell you? You will have to ask his majesty.

Mbing

I disagree with this? Do you know what you are unearthing?

Tawong

Yes

Mbing

What?

Tawong

Peace, love and respect for a brother king and his kingdom.

Mbing

No. This cannot be?

Tawong

Why?

Mbing

This is not a brother King?

Tawong

So who is he?

Mbing

This is a captive king. When you vanquish someone in war, you do not turn around and empty your barn of war booty. It is a war and whoever loses, loses and bears the consequences.

Tawong

Except this was not like any regular war.

Mbing

Yes it was! A war is fought by people who are determined to kill each other.

Tawong

But this was a war fought to peel off a brother's hand from our back.

Mbing
You mean we did not go to war to kill and win?
Tawong
Yes, but only to teach a brother a lesson, and get his hands off our back
Mbing
Forget this brother thing! If he was brother enough why were we fighting him?
Tawong
Can you tell me how much of his territory we took ever since we defeated him? Just show me. The only thing was to push him back so he never threatens us again.
Mbing
You are still not explaining to me how we are returning Sanguv to Momban, and why no one had respect enough for my family to just let me know.
Maa
(Dropping his staff and moving over straight to console Mbing)
I could not help over hearing you as I came through the brushes.
Mbing
So you are rushing in here only to tell me how noisy I am? Listen, I am the son of the Kah', one of the thirty aboriginals of this land and no one is going to trample on my right to have my right! It is my right to know.
Maa
Mbing, I am with you. How could Tawong or Yewong, or the Fon for that matter, our Fon, not even cough about this to us? I am not sure that even Faa knows.
Tawong
Telling anyone was not what I had to do.
Mbing
It was still a wrong decision. I have to tell the Fon that he has made a wrong decision that this kingdom may pay for dearly.

Maa

We are going together

Faa

We are going together

(They Exit. Ngaiwir, and the children appear from the hide out to comment before taking their positions again as the next wave of travellers come in.)

Tatah

How could they not inform Mbing and Faa and Maa? That was surely a mistake.

Menang

It seems that it was, but do you see how much they had to struggle with if they informed these people long ago?

Tatah

That would have helped them to resolve the matter before now.

Menang

That is what you think. May be it is not often easy to resolve issues between leaders. I have seen my father here disagree with our Shufai Sov, on some issues for the longest time. They could go on forever.

Tatah

You mean they quarrel a lot?

Menang

Not a lot, but they do not agree that often. Never!

Tatah

I wonder how they rule the place with that so much disagreement. That is bad.

Menang

May be disagreeing is not that bad; what might be bad is agreeing on the wrong things.

Ngaiwir

Alright children, that is enough. Sit over there and remain very quiet. *(Children exit)*

Menang

But father, where is the father of Mbing clan going with this?

Ngaiwir

I may disagree with him, but I think he should let the Fon know exactly how he feels.

Tatah

Are there some things the Fon does not need to tell everyone, like the things concerning what he does with other....

(Royal horn sounds indicating royal presence)

Ngaiwir

Here comes the Fon. Let's step aside and watch what happens.

Notes

1. Ntamirr:

   Ntamirr is a junction area understood to be the crossroad for all human and spiritual forces. Legend holds that God could disguise in human form and run all kinds of test on the living especially at a Ntamirr. Therefore having enough drink at a Ntamirr on such a day was crucial because He might show up thirsty and not have what to drink, in a land that He has so abundantly blessed.

2. Sealed-bag:

   Literally, 'bag without outlet': Refers to a bag whose content cannot be seen except by the buyer/owner and at his home. The concept of a sealed bag in Nso culture falls in line with a general practice among the grass field people of Cameroon who hold that some sacred items are bound by truth and therefore cannot be falsified, or modified. The bag is made with the content inside and at the end, there is no access created. Lack of an outlet or inlet is a symbol of sacredness.

Scene Four

(The Fon's entourage enters and Mbing is being hustled in front with Maa and Faa, but Mbing is making his point aggressively)

Mbing

(Strenuously)

I disagree, your majesty! This is the day that we, the children of Ngon, our founder, gather at the Rock to give thanks to The Builder for protecting us against our enemies and for providing us the prosperity that we have. This is not the day to celebrate with our enemies!

Faa

Your majesty, on this day we honour our heroes and relive our dashing moments in all battles from Tikari to this place. Ngon told us to make peace with those who want peace, but give our enemies to Nyuymbom[1] at his Rock to deal with. Instead, we are hurriedly hugging our enemies and bringing them to the greatest feast in our land?

Ndzev

I object to the way we are behaving in front of the lion of this land. Let me tell both of you that Momban is bitter about their King who never returned – the one we are still keeping. Traditionally, this means their king is still rotting in the battle field and needs to be buried. After all the love and brotherliness they have shown us over the years , they cannot understand what is making it so difficult for us to understand that our continuous keeping of this skull means the annihilation of their kingdom.

Mbing

Oh let them cry! They are playing the chameleon! That is how they are! They will serve us pelted stones for

35

an evening meal! As soon as they have their skull, they will create another reason to attack us.

Ndzev

But times are changing, my brothers and we cannot continue to live in fear or in the past.

Maa

Listen to you! Since when did we start going to bed with Momban? They have only started from this, but they will come for their children and cattle and artefacts we took when Momban fell.

Mbing

At peace, your majesty, we must always prepare for war. That is the strength of great nations.

Maa

The moment they ask us to return their women, that would be the beginning of fresh trouble. Are we ready?

Tawong

Your majesty needs to speak to our clan heads here. They do not seem to see anything else except a threat.

Mbing

And belittlement! No one would even inform us, keepers of the palace, about such a serious change in our relations with these Momban people. Why?

(The Fon lifts up his staff abruptly and the talking stops sharply. He coughs and addresses the issue)

The Fon

My elders and custodians of this land,
We do not ask a leopard why it has spots.
We just understand it has no choice in the matter.
Would I allow the eagle to visit my chicks?
That would be foolish!
Why would I want a hyena to raise my sheep?
If a brother is already on the ground,

36

Where else would you push him to fall?
Momban is our brother.
We share the same blood
And have a knot with them in addition.
What you are angry with is my word that I gave them.
That is where I took shelter
When it rained on my young years in Bamkov.
Many things happened when I was there.
This breath of good air was born then.
So let none reject them out of fear,
Or fear them out of rejection.
From the moment Bamkov put me
On the throne of Ngon-Bamkov[2],
And Momban put Njoya on Nchare-Yen's throne,
Hurricanes stopped building against us from the east.
Even Momban's love with Fonkimbang[3]
That captured kingdom upon kingdom,
Extending the borders and influence of Momban,
Now melts when the enemy they must face is Bamkov.
A brother comes to a brother for shelter,
Not to seek his head or burrow his walls,
So Njoya told Fonkimbang.
Fonkimbang, that red-lipped pitiless eagle
Cannot face Bamkov without Momban.
Fonkimbang cannot stand between us anymore.
When a brother shows you that he is brother,
Do you turn your back?
(Looks at everyone in the face and leaves quickly without another word)

Ndzev

Mbing, Faa and Maa, remember Fonkimbang?
Remember Kimforkir ke Chisong[4]?
What a sad day for our people,
But what a proud day it was too.
Fonkimbang who lived in Chisong,
Requested the presence of the lion of Bamkov.

You know what Fonkimbang asked him?
Will you stop fighting me and my people?
How can you stop fighting someone
Who wants to take over your land, and your property?
Who wants to take over your wives and your children?
How can you stop fighting someone
Who does not say anything that you understand?
He speaks through the nose,
And mumbles to his followers all the time
Even when talking with you.
He suspects you when you move to the side;
He suspects you when you dance, drink or eat.
He suspects everything you do,
And has scorn written all over his face.
He does not want to discuss with you.
He wants you to do everything he says;
He threatens to punish you and your subjects
If you do not do what he orders.
How can you work with a man
Who has so little regard for you and your people?
Well, our young fon, warrior of the first order,
Whose exploits turned his crippled legs[5] into legend,
Laughed at Fonkimbang in Chisong.
He laughed so loud that the ground quaked
And the roof almost came down on them.
Then bending down, the fon scooped up a handful of sand,
Raised up his hand and let the grains
Run down slowly through his fingers.
He asked Fonkimbang if he could count those grains of sand.
Fonkimbang shook his head in denial.
Well then, the fon said, that is how my people number!
And no matter how long the war lasts,
I will drown you up like a flood.

This Fonkimbang, we hear came from Jaman[6],
The place where warriors boil anger and drink like
soup.
Fonkimbang took just a sip from his steaming cup
And turned red, so red he moved from side to side.
Then he faced the young king with his smoking mouth,
And ordered the fon to declare the end of the war or die.
The fon laughed at him for saying that the fon could die.
So he told Fonkimbang that he chooses to disappear[7]
It is rumoured that he was forced to do the traditional
thing[8]:
We do not know if he drank a poisonous concoction
Or hung from tree top like a kola nut.
But people of Bamkov were summoned to collect
his remains.
(Takes a deep breath)
That is Fonkimbang for you.
That is the tarantula you have if you turn your back
on Momban.
That is the hungry lion who just wants meat no matter
how bitter it is.
He is fearless and moves around with a short line of
men,
Men carrying nuzzled short bamboos on their
shoulders.
When troubled, they point the nuzzle at the target
And it releases a loud sound like thunder in a cloud
of smoke.
When the smoke clears, a number of people lie dead
in their blood
With holes in their heads and stomachs.
I tell you, fathers of our clans, Fonkimbang is
merciless!
He smiles at you but still points his coughing bamboo.
That is the mark of someone who eats from both sides
of the hand.[9]

You cannot trust him!
If our Fon, the lion of this land, terror of the hills,
Says the spring Fonkimbang drank from with Momban
has dried up
I think we should believe him and welcome it!
When our majesty tells us that if Fonkimbang attacks
Bamkov or Momban
He will fight the two kingdoms together
I think we should welcome it!
Did he reveal all of this to us before?
He did not.
But does that mean that he has ceased loving us?
No!
Can any of us say he loves Bamkov less?
I do not think so.

Tawong

That is well said Ndzev. We have time and this event
to prove the Fon wrong.

Mbing

I do not question his love for Bamkov; I question the
decision he made. You never sleep with Momban
people with both eyes closed.

Faa

And when I look back, I am convinced they fought
us out of spite. To them we should not even be a
kingdom, since we are their sister's children. Our land,
according to them, is theirs.

Ndzev

That time is long gone.
Now we both are facing Fonkimbang
So we are working together.
You all go now and prepare for the start of festivities
at noon.
Momban should arrive by that time.
I will get there with his majesty.
(Ndzev exits, but Mbing, Faa and Maa plot strategy.)

Maa

I am not sure we can let things just happen the way Ndzev and the others describe. If their plan turns out wrong, this kingdom may see the greatest war surprise it has ever seen. Can we check with Mformi Bah and Mformi Gham for the latest border situation?

Faa

It does not seem to me that there would be much. I know I question the wisdom of the Fon in returning the skull of Fon Sanguv of Momban, but I do not have any reason to doubt that we are safe.

Mbing

I am sure our manjong is ready especially with the crown of Momban coming in. What I suggest we do is wrestle out the sealed-bag from leaving our land.

Faa

How are we going to do that? It has been blessed by Yewong and Tawong and treated by the royal cemetery earth-mother. Everything that is supposed to be done right has already been done. That is the reason we have the sealed bag. It would be torn open only in Momban and by the rightful people at the right location in their palace.

Mbing

If I let this happen, more than half of my family runs the risk of disappearing tomorrow when Momban comes for its children, their children and the entire progeny. You know how much loot and women we brought? I wish I had the chance to discuss this with the Fon, but he ignored me. He showed me and my family our nothingness. This is personal!

Maa

He also showed me and my family that we do not matter!

Faa

He showed me and my family that we do not exist.

41

Maa

This is personal!

Faa

This is personal! But how do we go about this?

Mbing

We set our children who are serving as guards and pages in the inner court on duty. Let them replace the sealed bag entirely, or just take it away.

Maa

That would be tough. But I will try to rally my boys.

Faa

Me too.

Mbing

Let us get to work.

(Exit)

(Children's voices come through as the children and Ngaiwir appear from their hide out.)

Tatah

Stop pinching me, Menang.

Menang

Who is pinching you?

Tatah

It is you!

Menang

(Mimics)

It is you!

Ngaiwir

Quiet, children!

Tatah

But old one he is bothering me

Menang

Who is bothering you?

Tatah

You!

Menang

You are the one bothering me!

Ngaiwir

Alright, alright children.

Tatah

How can they be preparing to do this?

Menang

They will just ruin the occasion if their plan works.

Ngaiwir

You people keep quiet!

Tatah

How can we, old one? We have been waiting for so long in this place. We have been out since night, waiting in this place to join Nwerong on its way to declare festivities open, but these people are only talking and talking and talking, and creating more trouble.

(Gwei enters in haste and goes to get a sip from the calabash of palm wine. Ngaiwir surprises him)

Ngaiwir

Who is that?

Gwei

(Startled, but realizes it is Ngaiwir)

Ngaiwir Tabesov, I hope you are on the way to the Rock, and not violating the laws of the land by squirrel hunting.

Ngaiwir

It is still morning and people are still on their way. Remember we decided to hold our steps back for a while so that when we leave here, it will not be long before festivities start at the Rock.

Gwei

I just returned from the Rock to pick up a few items from the fon's Mantum Shelter[10.] The festival ground is already filling up.

Ngaiwir

(Ignoring children)

I wish we knew where the Momban king is at this point.

Gwei

He is on the way I think.

Ngaiwir

But how far?

(Faint sound of palace bugle can be heard)

Gwei

Is that a faint bugle sound I am hearing? That means they should be somewhere around Kupa Matapit

Ngaiwir

That is too far for the sound to be heard at all. It does not show urgency for someone who has something this important to take home, if what we have been hearing here is true.

Gwei

You have been listening a little too much, Ngaiwir!

Laughs

Ngaiwir

Well, the Fon has eight hundred eyes ...

Gwei

And ears!

(They laugh, and then Gwei picks up a sound)

I can hear the faint sound of a palace bugle again. Can you hear it? Come closer here. Yes, they must be somewhere after Kitupirr or even in Ber[11]. That would mean very close.

Ngaiwir

No, the bugle sounds like that of a palace at rest[12]. Let us hurry to the Rock then.

Gwei

You would not wait for Nwerong again?

Ngaiwir

Not when Momban is already as close as the bugle sounds.

Gwei

I can only be happy to have your company back to the Rock.

Ngaiwir

The children have missed a great opportunity to travel in that massive group of branch-carrying Nwerong troupe chanting along in double-bell music like a giant forest moving on legs.

Gwei

Well, they will do it next time.

Tatah

When is next time, royal Gwei?

Ngaiwir

What do you mean by when is next time?

Gwei

I think he is referring to the next time the land goes to the Rock.

Ngaiwir

Victory day?

Gwei

Victory day! Let us go.

Exit

Notes

1. Nyuymbom:
   Literally, God the builder.

2. Ngon-Bamkov's children:
   Historians record that Ngon-Nso refused to be fon. Reasons
   for this are unknown, but the general sense is that she might
   have refused to be fon because she was a princess of the
   Tikari dynasty where it was not the custom for women to
   accede to the throne. She acted as regent for her son who was
   at the time of the treaty with the thirty aboriginals (Nso-Mntarr),
   underage.

3. Fonkimbang:
   Literally, 'king/fon of the redman' or king of the whiteman.

4. Kimforkir ke Chisong:
   Literally, the broken pumpkin of the Station. Station (Chisong)
   refers to the Bamenda station where the German colonial
   administrator built his residence, the German forte. History
   says that the Fon of Nso was forced into suicide because he
   refused to end the war he had waged against the German
   colonizers.

5. Crippled legs:
   Historians also reference a fon of Nso who was a cripple,
   but very deadly in war, and would appear at the war front in
   a rather unexpected manner.

6. Jaman:
   Lamnso for German or Germany

7. Disappear:
   In Nso worldview, the Fon like the sun, never dies. It sets and
   rises cyclically, so when the fon dies, the sun is said to have set
   on the land. When a new one is enthroned, the sun is said to
   have risen and is shining on the land.

8. Traditional thing:
   Suicide

9. Eats from both sides of the hand:
   Metaphorical expression for flip-flopping. This means someone who cannot be trusted.

10. Mantum Shelter:
    Refers to the current palace of Mantum, first constructed as a rest house for the fon during his hunting exercises in Dzekwa.

11. Kitupir or even in Ber:
    Kitupir is a Bamoun village bordering the kingdom of Nso on the south eastern frontier. It is currently settled by Nso indigenes and is bordered on the Nso side by the of Ber.

12. A palace at rest:
    When a traveling fon takes a rest before continuing his trip.

Act Two

Scene One

(Clearing in the bush: The background is all green and shrubby, reflecting the lush vegetation brought by rain. Tav is near a brook trying to get some water to drink. Princess Ngon tip-toes from behind the thicket)

Ngon

How is my Tav enjoying the great trek?

Tav

(Startled by the voice; turns sharply with his hand to his scabbard.)

What are you doing here! You frightened me. And I could have hurt you.

(Calmly advising)

You know that tradition does not approve that you come close to me until your bride price is fully paid.

Ngon

Well, I do not think his majesty has a problem with me being away as long as he knows that I am with you.

Tav

It is not about the Sultan; it is about tradition.

Ngon

He is tradition himself!

Tav

No, I do not want to be flogged! I do not want to be thrown into the Ngomba dark house by someone who does not know me or who just hates the fact that a Bamkov man is marrying their princess.

Ngon

Who does not know you in Momban? People here do not even think of you as a man from elsewhere.

Tav

It is unbelievable how far our people have come: From two quibbling siblings to the most trusting brothers.

Ngon

Trusting? The suspicion between the people is hard to overcome.

Tav

Well, we cannot help that. People are people and until they are part of something, they always doubt it, suspect it, disagree with it, or hate the outcome.

Ngon

I tell you, this morning in the palace…heh! His majesty could not believe how much suspicion and doubt there is in our kingdom about Bamkov.

Tav

This morning?

Ngon

Some of the advisers even wanted him to send his Mfuh warriors ahead to the Bamkov border. He said it would happen over his dead body.

Tav

I think he was right to be angry, and not send Mfuh.

Ngon

Yes, he was so angry at the suggestion that the palace quaked and Ngomba talked[1]. Then he walked over the ritual threshold in the cemetery of his fathers, placed the crown on the ground and asked all his Mfuh leaders to cross over it, in oath of allegiance to him and the kingdom.

Tav

He did that? He went that far!

Ngon

Yes, and doing so informed the leaders that he could never go back on his word to his brother, and that they should be ready to defend Bamkov any time Bamkov was attacked by just anyone.

Tav

That is something. Anger can sometimes push us to points of no return.

No wonder the feast of Ngon is going to happen with both kings present.

Ngon

Yes, in his anger he told his Mfuh leaders that if they did not want to bury Ngon his sister a second time, they should lay down their fear and suspicion.

Tav

Fear and suspicion!

Ngon

The true potions that weaken love and respect. He told them he named me, his daughter, after his sister as his way of confronting the horrific past of bloodletting between siblings. He told them that Momban would never again raise its hand over Bamkov, and that if Momban does, it would gradually disappear like the rays of a setting sun, never to be seen again.

Tav

Yes. Ngon founded the kingdom of Bamkov. And their brother founded Bashua. Their story is called the legend of the three siblings.

Ngon

That is what his Majesty keeps repeating: His sister's children, he would call Bamkov. And very recently, he has become very emotional about it.

Tav

Now go back before his majesty starts wondering what has happened to you. I am sure he is as unsure as everyone about this rainbow.

Ngon

He is, and is rather sullen.

Tav

Has he said a word yet?

Ngon

Not before I stole myself away.

Tav

Well, whatever is not right will burst the seams somehow.

Ngon

I think it will. Before I go back, here is a new porcupine spike for your cap.

Tav

It is not His Majesty's, is it?

Ngon

No, it is not!

Tav

Where did you get it?

Ngon

I do not go to the Ngomba house[2]

Tav

I know that.

Ngon

I do not enter his Majesty's sleeping chambers.

Tav

I know that too.

Ngon

You know everything then.

Tav

Everything that is Momban tradition.

Ngon

But it is still a very beautiful spike for your cap.

Tav

It is tough and shinny.

Ngon

I bought it in the market.

Tav

Market?

Ngon

From the man who delivers them to the palace.

Tav

He accepted to sell it to you?

Ngon

Only because I told him it was a gift for a male.

Tav

And he did not find out who the male is?

Ngon

I was not going to lie if he asked me. Princesses do not lie.

Tav

I am happy he never asked.

Ngon

I am just happy I was able to have it.

Tav

This will make me look like a prince.

Ngon

You are. You will soon marry the founder of Bamkov.

Tav

(Excited. Puts the spike in his cap, then mimics manjong dance; then dances out. Ngon watches him in admiration. Exits after him.)

Notes

1. Ngomba talked:
   When Nwerong or Ngomba music is played. When the music climaxes for a while, it could be referred to as 'standing' or 'talking'. The expression implies that the situation the music is played about is very serious.

2. I do not go to the Ngomba house:
   Ngomba is a male society, so access is not allowed to women. Since she does not have access, she surely could not have taken such a nice porcupine spike from there.

Scene Two

(Green and shrubby vegetation: Sultan sits in a shade. His party sits in semi circle around him. They are taking a rest from long hours of trekking. Mopete, his praise singer tries to nudge the sultan into mirth.)

Mopete

I am your majesty's praise singer
The proud song bird that welcomes the waking day;
The chanting voice singing joy into the royal heart;
My king sits peacefully like the rising sun,
And the world bends to his mighty fist.
Pride of our kingdom!
Strength of our men!
Lord of our land!
Wonderful father!
Revered emperor!
Precious King!
It is sunshine!

Mefiri

(Expressing a sense of urgency)
Mopete, take this for your peanuts today.
(Hands him money and Mopete exits Addresses the Sultan)
Your majesty, we have word that our journey may be fruitless!
(Sultan remains unmoved)
Your majesty, we have word that our father may not be retrieved on this trip.
(Sultan unshaken)
Your majesty we have word that Bamkov is not ready to give us your father to bring back for proper burial among his fathers.

Mominyi

(Panting)

Yes my lord, we have been informed by our eyes on the ground that as recently as this morning, there has been a lot of disagreements about letting us bring back our father for proper internment. What I suggest is that we be prepared for the worst.

Matapi

Indeed your majesty, there is nothing to live for if we cannot live for this. Your honour, your power, your glory all hang on this.

(Pause, waiting for a reaction from the Sultan)

Mefiri

Would not your majesty even say a word? All we need is your word and our fighters will mass up on the boundary.

Matapi

Mopete, may be you can help us prick the royal mouth. Your majesty surely needs his spirits enlivened to address the matter.

Mopete

Majestic Emperor!

Owner of our lands!

Warm blood running in our veins!

It is our majesty I greet,

And praise like my fathers did,

Warming the royal heart like my forebears.

This is the sun bird that sings my king into the royal sunbath.

I sing of my lord who descends from conquerors.

I sing of terror of kingdoms in the open savannah.

I sing of the sunshine that warms the people's blood.

Why would a dog not wag its tail at a gift of bone?

Why would it not lick the master's feet to make him smile?

Your singing bird is here with a cup of royal jokes,
Ready to warm your inwards:
(Sultan stare remains distant)
Remember the story yesterday my Lord;
The one about the prince of Tadu,
Captured with his young bride
While they were naked in the brushes!
Remember him running and heaving
His long whip from thigh to thigh?
The mad woman called it the third leg.
Now … even now… I can return
For the royal heart is warmed.
My Lord's teeth now shine
Like lightning in the night.
Our majesty, our majesty!

Sultan

Mopete, Mopete, Mopete!
Son of Ndunguri[1]
Son of my father's praise singers.
You are a true son of your father.
You are a great gift to this kingdom.
Now leave us alone Mopete
That we may haggle the affairs of the land
While you get something to eat.
(Mopete leaves, very excited that he got his master to smile)
Now, Matapi, Mefiri, and Mominyi
Come closer and hear me clearly.
(Pause)
We left our palace and are now in Bamkov
But you want us to turn back just because we fear?

Matapi

That is not so, your majesty. We just have evidence
that we cannot trust Bamkov people. Many of them
do not want us to return with our father, after the
event.

59

Sultan

And your answer to that is war?

You want us to move our fighters to the boundary?

Mefiri

Not exactly, your majesty. We just want us to be cautious. If we cannot run with our knees, we better crawl fast enough.

(Mbombo enters)

Sultan

If it is a matter of war,

I discuss with Mbombo first.

Mbombo, when did you last report about our fighters?

Mbombo

That was yesterday morning, my lord.

Sultan

What was it about?

Mbombo

It was to make sure that as we step out on this great trek, our land, our people and our property remain safe.

Sultan

Was there any problem about this trip?

Mbombo

No, your majesty, except if your brother the fon goes back on his word.

Sultan

That is the point. His word!

I have his word. It is wrapped.

It is his leash, and it is mine too.

If we straddle it, we correct our step.

But if we cross it, we pay the price.

The river does not go looking for holes in its track.

It digs them.

The cow does not sit waiting for green grass.

It seeks it.

If you tell a man the colour of your undergarments,
You make yourself a fool.
The word! His word!
That is what counts.
Our oath is fresh in the earth.[2]

Mefiri

So where are we in all this now?

Mbombo

Your majesty just said that. You of course know that
if it came to war he would lead our fighters.

Sultan

Here is something I want all of you to keep in your
heads: The lion of Bamkov is my brother.
He is the son of my older sister.
That is not something you joke with.
We suffered on each others' spears already.
But that was the end.
No more will this happen again.
The lion of Bamkov has lived with us.
He understands our needs.
He shares our dreams!
He and I grew up together:
We ate from the same dish
And played together every day.
He and I are like twins.
Not even the fon of the white people can tell me
who my brother is.
He is my nearest support if ever the hawks come.
I am yet to see who can bend our back if he and I
stand together.
Today, we have chosen to stand together on the
strength of our word.
I asked him to expect us and to open festivities on
time at noon.
That was also my word.

61

And I must keep it.

Stand up and let us try to get there on time.

And let this be the last distraction we have.

We must continue on our way.

(Faint sounds of drumming are heard in the distant.
Sultan exits with Mbombo and Mopete; Others confer)

Mefiri

I am afraid if he says so, we have to oblige.

He is the last cock that crows in the land.

Matapi

No! We serve the kingdom, not the king.

Matapi

But you serve the kingdom when you serve the king!

Mefiri

Stop this! It could be seen as disloyalty.

Get your bag and let us start the climb.

Mominyi

Yes, if our actions are wrongly interpreted, we could
pay the ultimate price. Let us get on the road quickly.

Notes

1. Ndunguri:
   Understood to be a class of palace pages in the Bamun
   kingdom

2. In the soil:
   Legend holds that when great leaders signed pacts, they took
   an oath over a live animal that they buried as part of the
   commitment.

Scene Three

At the Rock of God

(A plain on a low plateau: A huge rock broken into two pieces is prominent in the background. A fig tree is growing in the middle of the pieces of rock. Three calabashes of raffia palm wine properly oiled and hoofed on a carrying bamboo case stand in the foreground. In front is a serving calabash with a fresh peace plant (kikeng) placed in its mouth. A cub of kola nut, cowries, cam wood, a bowl and clay dish are all positioned inside a little circular fence built only with freshly thrashed raffia palm stalks. The sultan of Momban and the fon of Bamkov are seated prominently. Gwei motions everyone to come closer, clears his throat and looks around as if to make sure that everyone is ready.
He takes a prominent position in the arena and blows his elephant horn. Ngaiwir speaks to the children)

Ngaiwir
Keep your ears up, children.
Menang
What does he want to say?
Ngaiwir
How would I know?
Usually he lays it all out like pumpkin seeds
And it is left for us to pick out the rotten from the good;
Or the big from the small,
And the twisted from the straight.
Tatah
So what do we do now?
Ngaiwir
Take our seat among the people.
Gwei
(Blows his elephant tusk and jumps, darts and skips and displays with his spear and machete in a dance of war. Then taking centre of the arena he addresses the king and the crowd.)

63

True as the Ngewir waterfall tumbles down
And feeds the plains below,
This is your Gwei, majesty, lion, leopard!
True as Nwerong watches over this land
And keeps evil away from our borders,
This is your Gwei, mighty-one-with-eight-hundred-
eyes!
I am nothing but your royal servant,
I am nothing but your loyal spy,
Running through enemy ranks,
And prodding the fiercest into laughter.
I am your chameleon warrior,
Serving the enemy good food,
And watching him burp with fullness!
I wait for him to tire and snore,
Before my spear puffs his bubbled belly!
I am your herald, your harbinger,
Running the length of battle
And bringing word to women and children
Holed up in caves and under rocks.
Mine is the voice that tells them
War has been lost or won.
I am the eye, one of your eight hundred!
And as Mbárr Mountain[1] wears its cap of white cloud,
Even when there is no rain in sight,
So must we maintain our path,
Even when we lose our sight.

Fon

Yes, rouser of the kingdom!
Storyteller of our land
The people are waiting.
And if you are ready,
Let the story begin.
Let our people

Tell their story
About our long trek
From Tikari to war

(Gwei motions everyone to come closer. He darts from one end to the other and then realizing they have all given him full attention begins to shout out one riddle after another as the audience thunders back the response in a rather formulaic manner)

Gwei
Ma' Ngán(d) oh! *(A riddle for you all)*
Crowd
Ndze Ngon! *(Ready for you in this land of Ngon)*
Gwei
A mó moo wiy am dze a?
(Did I look the way I am when I first came here?)
Crowd
Nkoy lang! *(Clay pot!)*
Tawong
Ngo' nyom-nyom yeh dzeka?
(What do you choose for your appetizer?)
Gwei
Ngo' Nyom-Nyom yem dze Shitong!
(I choose a song bird)
Crowd
Ngo' Nyom-nyom ye kpeh wum kpah!
(Your sweet appetizing bird is ready for you!)

Gwei
(Clears his throat. Crowd giggles. Kigha music plays softly in the background)
> A very, very, very long, long, long time ago,
> The king of a far, far, far, big, big, big, big country
> called Tikari disappeared[2].
> Do you know who was supposed to replace him?

65

Crowd

No-o-o-o!

Gwei

A tall, strong, handsome prince called Nchare-Yen!

Crowd

Ye-e-e-es

Gwei

But Mveing his brother by another mother was made King

Crowd

No-o-o-o!

Gwei

This Mveing had the anger of a boa constrictor!
He had the fury of a dry season cobra!
In anger, he could shred his enemy like a tornado!
As soon as he was enthroned, he went after everyone.

Crowd

Everyone?

Gwei

Everyone that he considered a threat to him.
That included Nchare-Yen.

Tatah

(Jumps up in the crowd)

I need just one spear and I will go after that Mveing.

Gwei

Not so fast, young man!
Nchare Yen and his brother Mfombam left.

Crowd

They left?

Gwei

They left the kingdom and went down toward the river.
Many people left with them.
Their elder sister, Ngon…

Ngon

His majesty says that is who I am named after.

Gwei

Yes, princess, if it is his word, it must be true.
Ngon wanted to leave with the brothers but they
refused.
They said she was already married.
A married woman belonged to her husband's home.
She did not belong to her mother's family anymore,
So it was not right for her to come with them.
She had to stay back with her husband and children.

Menang

(Jumps up a little frustrated)

But that was not fair. She could at least bring her
whole family along. She was not going to be safe in
the hands of this new Mveing king.

Gwei

Very good, young man!
She and her family could fall prey to Mveing's spear,
Because they were all children of the same mother
and father.
So she took her children and left after her brothers
any way.
She was a brave woman who knew what it meant to
be a mother.

Tatah

What about her husband? Did he stay? They could
kill him too!

Gwei

Well, I think he chose to stay
Because he had other wives
Who could cook for him and bear him more children.

Ngon

He behaved like the stupid mother deer that refused
its mate food and then became food for the lion. If
the sister and the brother face him, where would he
hide?

Gwei

Oh princess and founder,
It may truly be that you have come back
Under the watchful eyes of the Rock
To stop brother from slaughtering brother,
And show them the common enemy!

Sultan

Go ahead Gwei.
Let not a morsel drop
From this gigantic story.
For without it told in full,
We will only be fools
When our right arm slaughters the left!

Fon

Or when the left slaughters the right!

(Giggling in the crowd)

Mopete

If wisdom were water,
We would say our kings drink a lot of it!
If it were meat
We would say our kings eat too much of it!
It is hair
And builds its fence on top of their eyes
Or makes a forest on their head!
It could turn white, but does not go away.
Royal fathers, our sun is truly shining!

Gwei

And indeed it shone on Mfombam and Nchare-Yen
For they ran as fast as the leopard
Until the wind that blew hard stopped.
Once the brothers left the plains behind,
They stood on top of the hill to look back
To make sure the enemy was not on their trail.
But far in the distance they saw the stout image
Of their sister leading a horde of women, children
and men,

Heading in their direction and closing in on their heels.
The people behind her looked like a herd of cattle.
But Mfombam and Nchare-Yen feared to break tradition;
They feared the earth would haunt them
If they gave her company.
So they r-a-a-n,

Crowd

And r-a-a-n

Gwei

And r-a-a-n
And r-a-a-n
And crossed river Mbam.

Yewong

(Cutting in)

No, no, no. You are leaving out something important!
The River they crossed was called Mape.

Tawong

Yes, Mape. That is the name! Mape!
It flows into Mbam a little further down.

Fon

What is the difference?
Mape or Mbam disappears into each other,
And into the swamps that murmur into the endless lake.

Gwei

(Smiles broadly at the interjection)

Your majesty has a way of putting things…
He makes all difficult things sound so easy!

Mopete

Wisdom, comes with the royal sunshine!
Wisdom is the sun in our royal household.

(Royal bugle sounds briefly)

Yewong

Some brothers actually waged wars of capture
To arrest and take back their sisters to their husbands.

Gwei
Not these brothers, mother of our land.
They wanted their sister safe
But just feared the blame.

Menang
So what did they do?

Gwei
When they saw her still coming?

Crowd
Yes!

Gwei
They cut the bridge into the raging river.

Crowd
How Cruel!

Mopete
Nchare-Yen and Mfombam were clever.
Like fast warriors they sped downward
And battled the local men one after the other,
Swelling their numbers with fallen foes.
But Mfombam would not stay
To be ruled by his brother.
So he took a group of followers
And went warring further
Until tired he settled in Bashua.³
But Nchare-Yen,
The viper with a double head⁴,
Remained where their paths parted.
He levelled the valleys,
Silenced the hills,
Stormed the woods,
Broke the tough,
Burnt the enemies
And established his kingdom,
Then named it Momban
After his older brother, Mfombam.
My sultan is the blood of Nchare-Yen

Gwei

Ngon and her followers went up the river
In search of the fleeing brothers.
But the brothers had disappeared,
Disappeared like a drop of water in a river.
She stood on the hill and called out,
But her voice came back with mocking emptiness.
She searched, and searched, and searched, and
searched.
But gave up when fruitless turned the search.
She settled in Mboh, and then moved to Kovifem.
Her numbers shook the forests[5]
And aboriginals sued for peace:
Ngon's sons would rule the land
But whoever rules must be
Born of an aboriginal mother;
Born in the royal palace,
On top of the leopard skin.
For a time, Ngon lived in peace.
And her people worked like bees.
But war, why did wrath give you birth?
Oh war, why did selfishness deliver you?
You came upon mother hen
With the language of iron.
You came with machetes, spears and bows.
In your trail you left silence, fear and putrid stench.
In your trail you left hyenas, eagles and desolation.
You forced Ngon into Tavisa and then to Nkim-Mboh.
Since then Bamkov has never left.
Ngon's children have fought many wars:
With Momban, the children of Nchare….

Tata

If Momban and Bamkov are children of brother and
sister, born by the same father and mother, how come
when they found each other, they did not embrace
themselves, but fought and killed each other?

71

Fon

(Cutting in suddenly)

Whose child has asked that question?
Send the child forward!
Right up here!

Gwei

Sun of our land,
Shining on all of us
We pray that your love,
Not your wrath
May bless your son;
Your son, my king,
Son of Tabesov
Son of Bukap!

Fon

Bukap! You said Bukap?
Bukap! Our valiant Gwei
The gift of the Rock to Tabesov!
Bukap who went to war to bring us peace
But brought us a double bag:[6]
One bag full of sorrow and shame
And another full of pride and victory
All in one hand.
Son of Tabesov,
Your question answers our question today!

Sultan

How could a person shed his own blood?
The answer is the spark that lights our way:
First our tradition and custom said our sister
Could not have a kingdom while we live.
So as long as the sun rose and set,
We had to make it part of our Kingdom
So that we could take care of all our children,
And our children include her children.
Time had settled Nchare-Yen's fear[7] -
The fear that his sister belonged elsewhere.

So we extended spears and guns
To bring her under control.
Now we know that a hug was all we needed.
After all, no one shows warring strength in his
homestead,
Unless he wants defeat from his wife some day.
But in our blindness we waged war.

Fon

And Bamkov, Ngon's children answered!
We answered with spears and machetes.
How else could we have responded when
A brother who abandoned us in the hostile dark of night
Appears not to say he was sorry, but to slap and burn us?
Like a tadpole we were stuck to our water pool
But suddenly ruffled and kicked in the spine
By an aggressor who called himself brother.
We tried to make peace,
But they killed our men.
Mangled Bamkov turned to the one thing that worked:
We turned to this Rock,
And He gave us fangs
To devour Momban in one bite
If Momban hit.

Sultan

And Momban hit!
But it was all so selfish, so selfish.
We knew that Bamkov was red with anger,
But we still attacked.
Why did Nchare Yen's children do this?
Our young Sultan was worried
He may be overthrown by bully Mfuh leaders.
He started the war so they could all be killed fighting.
So how did he start the war?
He stole the wife of the Fon of Bamkov
Just to enrage a brother king
And Bamkov pounced on us like lions on mice

73

Fon

In the end, we all lost men and property.
Bamkov kept the head of king Sanguv.
But the ants that chase out a toad
Also chase out a rat!
Nwerong wanted my head:
They said I was born to rule,
In a sea of blood;
The blood of those
Who fared in intrigue.
They feared to die.
So they chose that I die!
Nwerong wanted my head in a mat
The mat that was seized in Tabesov,
Where I was also seized from their fatal grip.
I ended up like Nchare Yen, in Momban.
My brother here was a good companion.

Sultan

We grew up together.
The stars said it right:
One day you both will rule.

Fon

So we sought the justice of the earth

Sultan

In ending this endless rancour.

Fon

Between Ngon

Sultan

And Chare-Yen

Fon

Today, my brother must return with his father.

Sultan

And today it must be known,
That if one of us raise a hand over the other
He is cursed!

Fon

He is cursed!

Sultan

By the earth!

Fon

By the earth!

Sultan

That is all!

Fon

That is all!

(To Tatah)

Now, son of Tabesov
Successor of Gwei Bukap
This cap with the red feather is put on your head
As a sign of your assignment to this kingdom.
We will be here when you complete the elephant hunt
And bring your catch to the people.
Let the celebrations begin!

(Both potentates raise their staffs and gunfire rumbles off)

Notes

1. Mbárr Mountain:
    Prominent Mountain on the south-eastern frontier of Nso
    and Bamoun kingdoms. The mountain steeply faces the Nso
    plain of Ber and rolls off in a range that diminishes in height
    towards Foumban, the capital of Bamoun kingdom.

2. Disappeared:
    In Nso mythology, the death of a king is called a
    disappearance.

3. Bashua:
    This is a reference to Bafia which historians say was created
    by Nchare Yen's younger brother Mfombam, after they parted
    ways and Nchare founded Bamoun.

4. The viper with a double head:
   The double-headed viper is carved over the door post of the Bamoun palace in Foumban as a symbol of the deadly war-faring character of their kings.

5. Shook the forests:
   Frightened everybody

6. Double bag:
   Mixed blessings

7. Nchare-Yen's fear:
   Referring to the fear that if he acquiesced or aided the sister to run away from her husband, the laws of the land will convict him.

Scene Four

(The Sultan and the Fon are seated. Kirang ke Ngiri festival music is playing. Dancing by women clad in wrappers and men in multicoloured woven gowns is happening in the round. The mood is festive and the dancing is an integrated display of masquerades especially Mooh, Mohmvem, Wan-Mabuh and others. Masquerades dance to the monarchs and retreat to the circle. The monarchs salute each dance by getting on their feet and dancing briefly then regaining their seats. Tavnjong approaches Mformi Bah and Mformi Gham. They clang machetes in manjong customary greeting; Tavnjong thumbs up to both and they all dance in opposite directions. Then Mbing, Faa and Maa hold an undertone conversation by the side)

Maa

As planned?

Mbing

As planned!

Faa

Set!

Mbing

Sure?

Faa

Sure!

Mbing

Get busy!

Maa

(Seeming a little worried)
I am not sure how it will end

Mbing

Leave that to the Mighty One of the Rock. When the last masquerade dance is on display, we move!

Maa

His majesty will never forgive us for this.

Mbing

It is in the name of the people!

Faa

The same people he rules over!

Mbing

We are the people!

Maa

That sounds like he wanted to destroy the land and we rescued it.

Faa

Yes, but all we have done is protect our families from the erosion that the return of the captured sultan will initiate.

Mbing

Our families are the people and they must neither be eroded nor lose what is rightfully theirs because of a fon's secrete contracts with foreign kings.

Faa

We have got this one covered.

Maa

They may be looking at us. We better disappear!

(They disperse quickly. Music heightens. Dancing continues and occupies foreground. The crowd of dancers is raved, as dancing climaxes. The complexity of the festival is visible in both substance and mood.

Suddenly, Tawong, with a Nwerong masquerade in tow, rush in and Tawong throws himself on the ground in front of the Fon and Sultan. Both potentates stand up in amazement and shock. Tawong quivers irrepressibly. Nwerong masquerade stands by. Drumming and dancing stop dramatically. Silence!)

Tawong

Your majesty! Your majesty!

Fon

Yes Tawong, get up! On your feet!

Tawong

My lord, trouble…

Fon

Trouble…What trouble?

Tawong

Trouble has visited!

Fon

Visited who? Where?

Tawong

Visited us!

Sultan

What? Who is dead?

Tawong

No, your majesty!

Sultan

Then what Tawong?

Fon

Yes what?

Tawong

Darkness has fallen on your majesty's word!

Fon

Have I lied to anybody?

Tawong

No your majesty, only in a way!

Fon

Stop jumping over words and tell me exactly what the matter is!

Tawong

My lord may bite his tongue…

Fon

Only liars do, and I am not one! If there is nothing to say, go prepare our brother's departure and stop quaking and dribbling words like a thief.

Tawong

(*Shakes his head*)

No, your majesty. A terrible thing! An abomination, my king! The sealed bag has disappeared!

Fon

What do you mean the sealed bag has disappeared?

Tawong

Your majesty! The sealed bag that we took months to prepare is gone!

Fon

Gone where, Tawong? Did the bag just walk away?

Tawong

Missing, your majesty! Missing!

Fon

Stop messing with missing, Tawong! Missing how?

Tawong

Someone must have stolen it!

Fon

Stolen? Stolen? No one steals a king!

Tawong

I don't know what to suggest, my lord!

Fon

You don't know what to suggest! After how many years of safe keeping? Where were the guards? Where was everybody?

Tawong

The guards were there, your majesty!

Fon

Were they sleeping?

Tawong

They told me they were not!

Fon

Then they took it!

Tawong

They say they did not take it

Fon

Then who did?

Tawong

I cannot say, your majesty

Fon

So you know who did, but just cannot say!

Tawong

Leopard of the kingdom, I do not know who did.

Fon

(Moves frantically and regains position)

Can we have Yewong here!

(Yewong enters)

Yewong, I have summoned you because I have to do the unusual thing.

Tawong here reports that the sealed bag is missing.

Tawong admits that the guards never took it.

But Tawong says he does not know who took it. Are you aware of this?

Yewong

My lord, how could I not? Tawong and I have been busy on the search.

Fon

Who is robbing me of my word, Yewong?

Yewong

If I knew the answer, my king would have known already

Fon

Who wants my head?

Yewong

Not in this land! Not while the sun still rises over Tahyarr[1] and sets over Ngongbaah

Fon

Where are Mformi Bah' and Mformi Gham?

(Mformi Bah' and Mformi Gham enter)

Let everyone come closer here.

Summon everyone!

We have to face the truth

In front of the throne!

Tawong

Your majesty does not intend to make bad matters worse!

81

(As the Fon pulls out his sword from the scabbard and lays it on the ground in front of all, Tawong tries to restrain him)

Tawong
No your majesty!

Fon
Yes, Tawong!

Tawong
Let us search one more time

Fon
We do not have that much time

Tawong
Just another chance!

Fon
Why another chance?

Tawong
Just another try!

(Aside to Sultan)

I do not know what may be going through your mind now
My brother, but I see your children are on each others'
throat.
If you would speak to them, while I speak to these
here,
That may help me get to the bottom of this.

Sultan
The only thing I stand on is your word.
As long as I return with my father
It does not matter what trouble I go through to get
there.

Fon
You are a true brother, and I thank you over and over.

(Exits with Yewong, Tawong while Nwerong keeps watch as sultan and his people address concerns)

Sultan

Mbombo, this is not the time to let your temper get
the better of you.

Mbombo

It is him, your majesty.

Mefiri is telling me that if we had moved our fighters
close by, we would have swooped in and carried
everything here.

Mefiri

I am saying you have sold out Momban for peanuts.

Mbombo

You are back on it again?

Mefiri

Who would not? I tried to get you to understand that
we cannot trust these Bamkov people, but you would
not listen.

Mbombo

I would not listen?

Mefiri

Yes, if you had listened, we would not be here.

Mbombo

Our fighters are ready, but it is not everything that
you get by fighting.

Mefiri

You said His Majesty relied on Bamkov's word.
Whoever listened to that kind of talk?

Mbombo

Well, we did, and where we are is where we are. Until
we have heard the last word from Bamkov, we cannot
conclude anything.

Sultan

Yes, Mefiri. Momban is very proud of that fire in you.
Your love for your kingdom shows in that fire.
Let us allow Bamkov to finish its process.
I assure you I am not returning home without your
father.

The process may be uncomfortable, but you have to let it run its course.

Now take your places and let us see what Bamkov will do.

Fon

(Enters with Tawong and Yewong looking furious. Then suddenly intones a manjong song and the crowd answers in a roar of unison: then he begins)

People of Bamkov, people of Bamkov!
I am not sure which side my forebears are facing now
But what has happened is an abomination.
It is never done.
I saw the rainbow!
You also saw the rainbow.
And I must tell you this:
Rivers do not flow uphill!
The shoulder never grows taller than the head.
Today is the day we celebrate Ngon, our mother.
My brother and his people are here to celebrate.
They are here so we all can bury a past we all hate.
He is also here to take home the sealed bag.

(He bursts into manjong song and then stops abruptly then starts calling out)

The sealed bag! The sealed bag!
Sealed in word and deed!
Sealed with the blood of our ancestors;
Sealed with the truth they left us;
Sealed with the weapon of the Rock:
That boulder of truth that we turn to
When all else has failed us in Bamkov!
Bamkov! Bamkov! Oh Bamkov!
This land of warriors and conquerors!

Who has done this to you?
Who has changed the size of your tongue?
Who has sent you out in the middle of the night?
Who of you has moved Sanguv from among his
brothers?
(Scans his subjects with a painful and slow stare; then resumes)
　　I have asked you in plain Lamkov[2]
　　But have received silence in response.
　　When a river has nowhere else to flow
　　It breaks a wall and overflows its banks.
　　We have to move this matter away from our hands
　　And place it in the hands of the Mighty One of the
　　Rock.
　　Bamkov, may your truth save you.
　　May they who have done this face your wrath,
　　Mighty Builder who resides in this Rock
　　Bring the Rock forward!

(A replica of the bigger Rock is brought forward and placed at the centre of the clearing. A piece of the cloth on which previous fons sat is brought and placed over it. This should represent the first throne which Ngon held as regent for her growing son)

Faa
Your majesty, let us search more.
Maa
Yes my king, another search can unearth the bag.
Beating the throne is drastic.
Mbing
Very drastic! Too drastic!
Fon
We use drastic measures because we have to.
Line up behind Yewong, and Tawong, all of you.
Your truth will set you free
Put your hand on the Rock on which

Ngon first sat, and swear on your truth.
You must choose your own calamity.
Yewong, you start!

Yewong

May lightening strike me down
If I know who took the sealed bag:
Bag of the earth!
May the strike be sudden!

(*Places his hand on the stone throne for a brief moment and then moves over to the other side. Tawong moves forward*)

Tawong

I have served my fathers and our Kingdom
With child-like honesty.
I have worked with sincerity and utmost truth.
I continue to shed tears since I discovered this.
May Mbím and Mairin[3] separate if my word is not true.
May the hands of death shrivel me like a dry reed
And my body be discarded in the open field
To be eaten by wild dogs and crows
If I know who took the sealed bag:
Bag of the earth!
May the hands of death strike me while we are still here!

(*Places her hand on the stone throne for a brief moment and then moves over to the other side.*)

Mbing

(*Visibly shaken*)

My turn? My turn?
Let me turn!
Or give me a different turn.
Why are we doing this?

Fon

Stop wasting our time!
Just do what you have to do!

Mbing

Do you have to shout at me?
Your majesty is trying to push me!

Fon

No one is trying to push you.
No one has asked for that.
Your truth is your axe.
It will fall on your head
Or it will fall on the wood.
But it is in your hands.
Now hurry up!

Mbing

Your majesty just said, axe
Axe or ask!
Which is which?

Fon

Has he just gone mad?
What has happened to our chief executioner?

Mbing

Nothing, your majesty. Nothing!
The louse feasts on the head
But does not care if something else is feasting on it!

Fon

I am soon going to ask Nwerong to do its work.
You are beginning to be a piece of work!

Mbing

Now your majesty is saying he will force me!

Fon

Nwerong, get him to do his turn!

Tawong

(*Steps in*)

Not so soon my Lord.
He has to beat the throne willingly

87

He has to do so of his own free will
He cannot do it by force.

Fon

You mean Mbing will put the land on hold?
You mean we will watch him dance back and forth
Like a cricket that has heard foot vibrations
Without being able to do anything about it?

Faa

Besides, your majesty, he seems to have had too much to drink.

Maa

We seem stock then.

Fon

Can we not skip his turn, Tawong?

Tawong

Your majesty, we cannot.
The shoulders never grow taller than the head.
He is the Chief Executioner of the land.
He is the only hand that rises above the fon's head
When the Lion has started eating its own cubs
He must therefore be an example of living truth.
He must be sober when the land is drunk!

Fon

But now he is drunk when the land is sober!

Tawong

Yes, my Lord, but we must be careful how we handle him!
Even our roads are sometimes slippery.
That does not mean we stop using them.

Fon

(Screaming and agitated. Looking fierce)
No! No! No.......!
I am either the fon or I am not!
Am I living the fate of the proverbial hunter?
The one who was sent to hunt without the spears?
You ask me to plant and refuse me the grain?
Bamkov cannot do this to itself.
We must change it!

Tawong

G-r-a-d-u-a-l-l-y, my king, g-r-a-d-u-a-l-l-y!
We cannot change it just because we do not have our
way.

Fon

Tawong, you are under oath.

Tawong

That I know your Majesty.
I must balance what is quick and easy with what is
necessary.
For now, it is necessary to follow the laws of the land.
It is a tough journey, my lord.

Fon

Well, we just got to the end of the road.

*(Pulls out the royal cowries and lays them in front of the stone throne.
Takes off the royal necklace and bangle and lays them on the same
location.)*

I am ready to do the traditional thing!
If Mbing cannot bow to the laws of the land
And I cannot do anything about it
Then what use am I to this kingdom?
If my word can be trampled underfoot
In the public, in front of my eyes,
What use am I to the kingdom?
May be it is better I be known as
The broken pumpkin of Bamkov
Rather than the toothless king
That I am at the moment.
May be when I am no more here
The Mighty Rock will speak to Bamkov!

Tawong

Those are heavy words your majesty.
As you can see, it is not only the guards

Fighting their tears but the kingdom as a whole.
No, my king, the sun never sets on Bamkov at noon!
No your majesty, Mbing will have to drink
From his own cup of death if he refuses to beat the throne.
Give us a chance mighty king…just another chance!

(He signals Nwerong masquerades and guards and Mbing is hauled into the fore. Yewong comes forward with the cup of bitter fluid, and stands astride over it; then she incants)

Yewong

Eh Ngon Bamkov, mother of fertility, great nourisher,
Founder and mother of our kingdom.
You who preserved this kingdom for your progeny,
Rise now from your sleep and spew your anger.
Rise now and save the land from annihilation.
Our fingers are twisted by the rules you left.
Our thumbs are numb because of the work you left.
Our hands are tied because of your children.
Raise your head from your peaceful sleep and listen;
Listen to the children to whom you gave work but no hands.
Rise and do justice with your hand.
Let your anger boil through this juice.
Let him who drink it know that you made it
Let his journey be smooth and fast.
Founder of this land, take over so that I step back.

(She motions to Nwerong to bring Mbing forward. Mbing is pulled along and held tight and motionless. Yewong administers the ritual)

Nourisher, give him a chance to spare this land disaster.
Ngon-Bamkov, give him one chance to confront the truth.

Restore his voice, restore his strength; give him breath.
This is the liquid of justice; you made it for him,
But give him another chance.
Move in him, squeeze his balls,
Twist his neck, and turn his head.
Turn him upside-down,
And pour out that truth.

(Words start tumbling from Mbing's mouth. Yewong goes on with hard encouragement)

Mbing
It is not w-i...th..me..me...

Yewong
What is not with you?

Mbing
No..n-o-t..w-i..t-h...me-e!

Yewong
What is not with you?

Mbing
The b-a...ba-ba-bag!

Yewong
The bag?

Mbing
Ye..e..s-s-s!

Yewong
Which bag?

Mbing
Siiiiiiiilllllltttttt!

Yewong
Sealed!

Mbing
S-e-a-l..e-d b-a-b-a-g!

Yewong
Sealed bag?

Mbing

Se-al-ed bag!

Yewong

Where is it?

Mbing

Sar….kov..vv

Yewong

Speak clearly!

Mbing

Sarkov

Yewong

What is it doing in Sarkov?

Mbing

Hi-di-ng!

Yewong

Hiding from who?

Mbing

Mom-ban!

Yewong

Why?

Mbing

Fear!

Yewong

Fear of what?

Mbing

Fear of what Momban may do!

Yewong

Like what?

Mbing

Like ask for other things we took after we won the war.

Yewong

Other things, like what?

Mbing

(Tearfully)

My great-grand mother was one of the girls captured!

Yewong
You fear because you may be asked to return her?
Mbing
Yes, and what would I do?
Yewong
You fear because there is nothing to give back to them?
Mbing
Yes, except everyone in my family now, including me!
Yewong
Where did you hide the sealed bag in Sarkov?
Mbing
With Wulem Kimbóv
Yewong
Tawong, dispatch Nwerong!

(Drops the ritual accoutrements back in the calabash container then addresses the rest of the people in court)

We have all seen and heard.
We are all witnesses to the truth.
We must watch out for what is happening.
Have you seen what fear alone can do?
Darkness almost hit us in the middle of the day
Because of fear
We almost broke our kinship bridge
Because of fear
The Fon almost declared a broken pumpkin
Because of fear
Bamkov almost lost control of its truth
Because of fear
Momban almost went back without their prize
Because of fear
Our hierarchy almost broke down
Because of fear.
Fear is the only enemy we have in this land,
For the rulers as well as the ruled

It is fear that has torn our trust to shreds
It is fear that has mangled our conscience
And if we let it, fear will bury us alive.

(Spotless brown Nwerong masquerades enter carrying the Royal Sealed Bag in a long White and Black coloured bamboo pole. Yewong issues an ululation of victory and orders the fon to his feet and the Momban train unto the foreground)

Rise up my majesty, my fon, my elephant, lion of Bamkov!
Rise up, mighty beast that tramples down our thick bushes,
Rise up I say and put the royal sword in its scabbard.
Hold your staff, great king, successor of Ngon-Bamkov
And lead your brother to the boundary fig tree.
Mformi Bah, Mformi Gham, give your majesty his deserved salute!

(They clang machetes with him)

Gwei, let the earth shake with your horn!
Mopete, let the sultan's bugle sound from Mairin to Mbam.
Let it drown the passing wind.
Let the music be heard in the heart of Momban country
Because today, the word has conquered the world,
And his majesty your great-grand-father is travelling home.

(Yeh Nwerong[1] files along graciously as ladies and the jubilating crowds sweep the path with their hands, in joy and ululation. Manjong music dominates the scene. Evening gradually descends on the land as the Momban train starts out.)

END

Notes

1. Tahyarr:
   A hill that rises steeply behind the palace of Nso in Kimbo and stretches across the Shisong neighborhood to the Mbuluv ranges.

2. Lamkov:
   Language of Bamkov

3. Mbím and Mairin:
   The two legendary rivers in ancient Nso. They flow in the north-east of the Kingdom. They empty their waters into the river Mbam.

4. Yeh Nwerong:
   A major palace dance often executed in grace, linear match pass, and slow gait. It is one of the dances where pride is exercised during a festival occasion. Membership into the dance group is seen as a sign of achievement and success.